GUITAR ANTHOLOGY
CREED

C000062821

ALBUM ARTWORK

My Own Prison © 1997 Wind-up Entertainment, Inc.

Human Clay © 1999 Wind-up Entertainment, Inc.

Weathered © 2001 Wind-up Entertainment, Inc.

Alfred Publishing Co., Inc.
16320 Roscoe Blvd., Suite 100
P.O. Box 10003
Van Nuys, CA 91410-0003
alfred.com

ISBN-10: 0-7390-5567-4
ISBN-13: 978-0-7390-5567-0

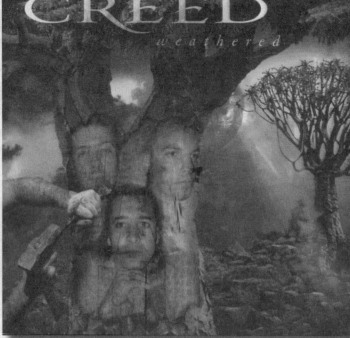

CONTENTS

ARE YOU READY?

Words and Music by
MARK TREMONTI and SCOTT STAPP

Are You Ready? - 5 - 1

6

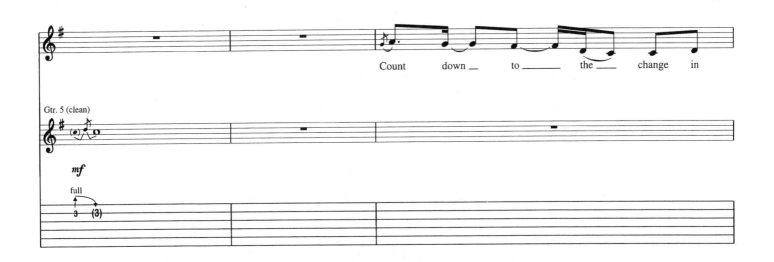

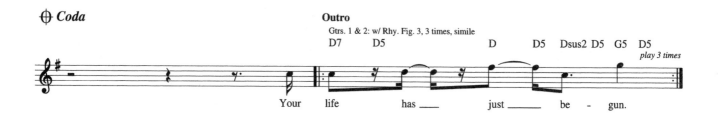

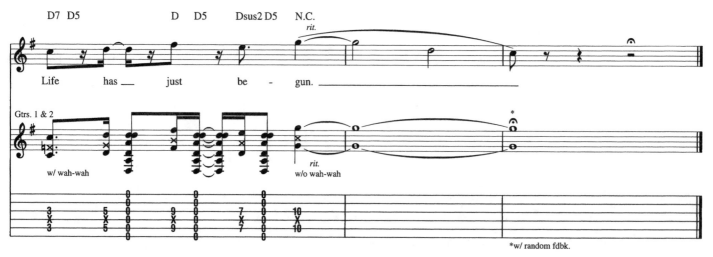

FACELESS MAN

Words and Music by
MARK TREMONTI and SCOTT STAPP

1. I _____ saw a face spent a day _____ on the wa- ter. _____ by the riv- er. _____

I It looked

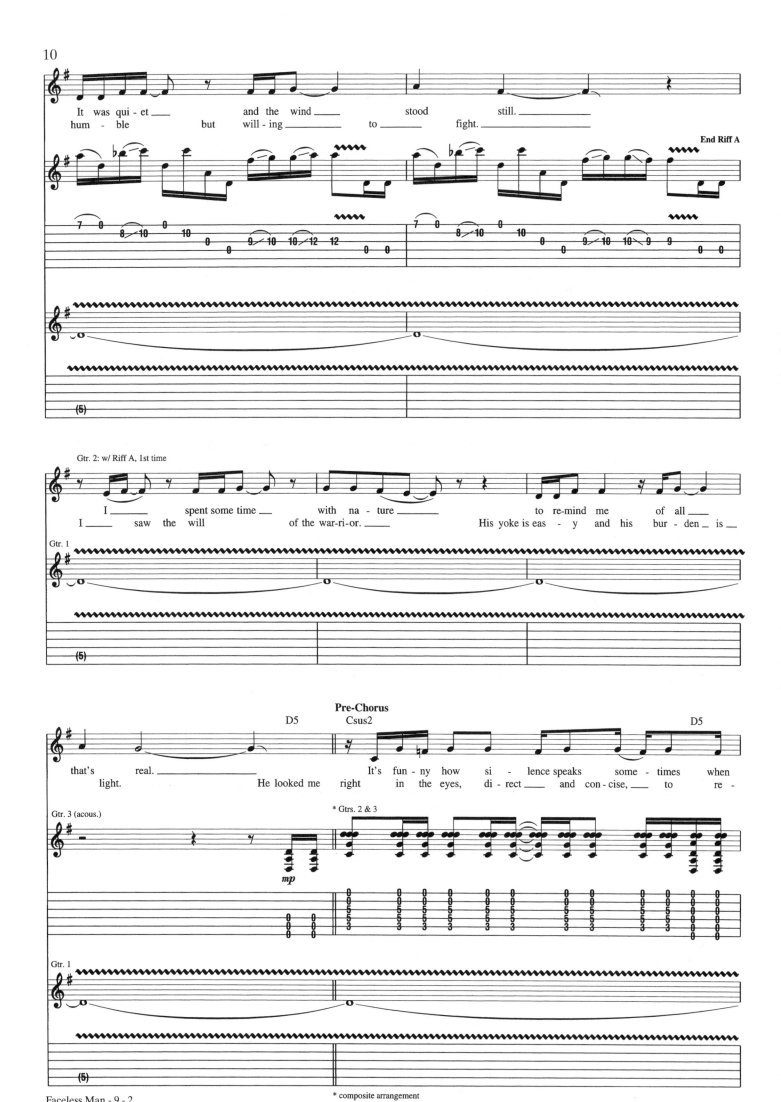

* composite arrangement

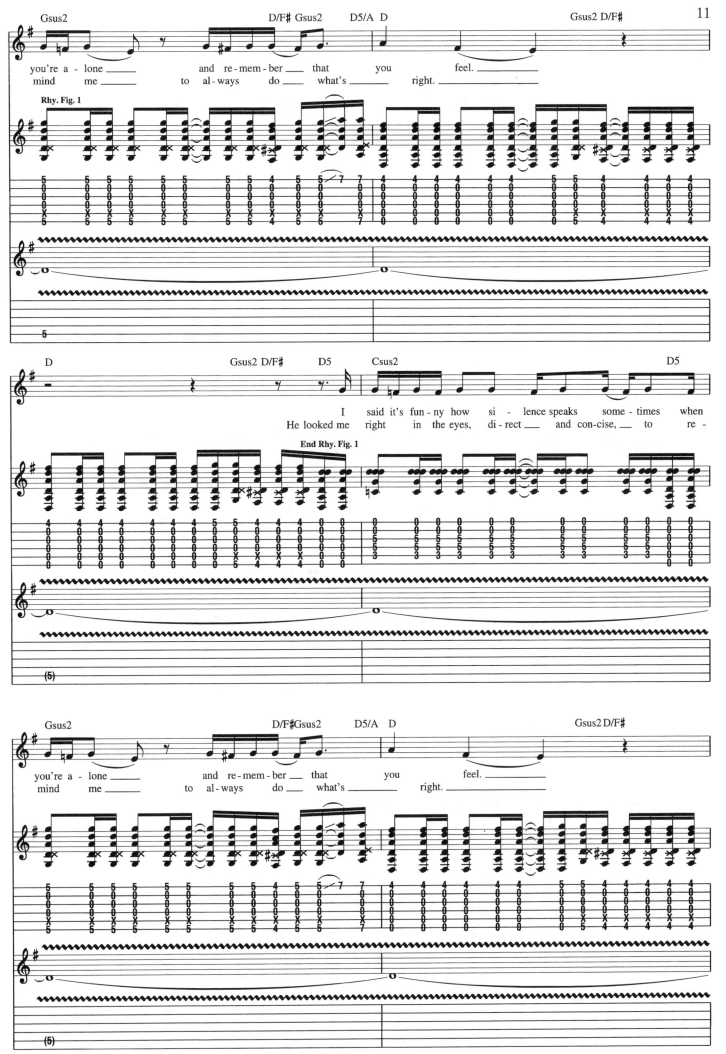

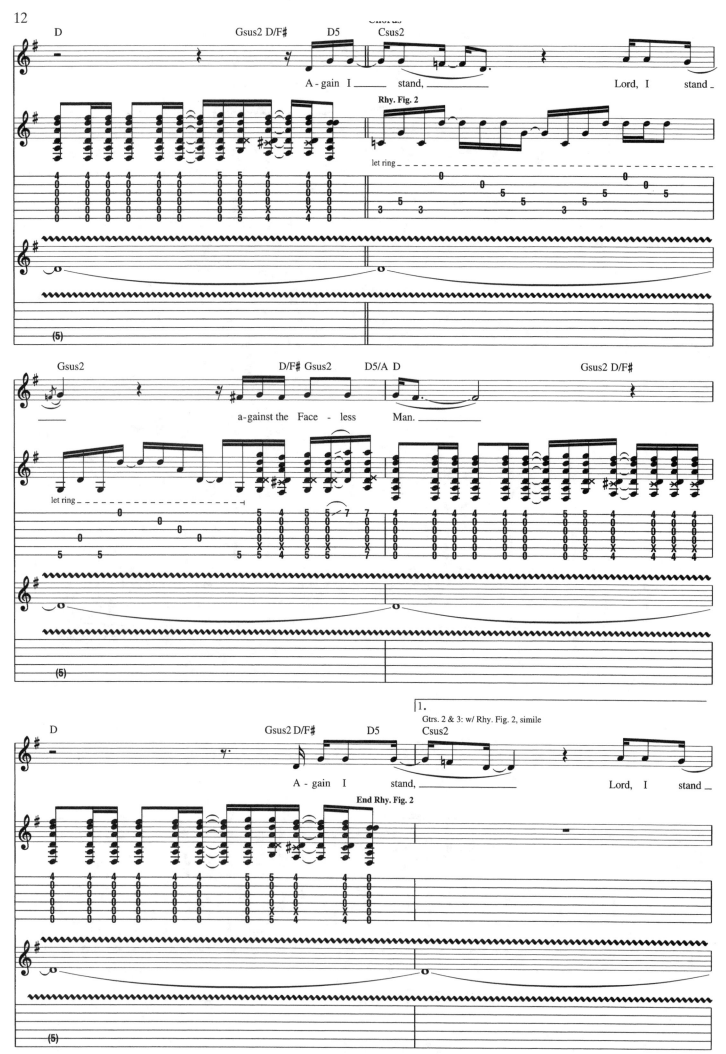

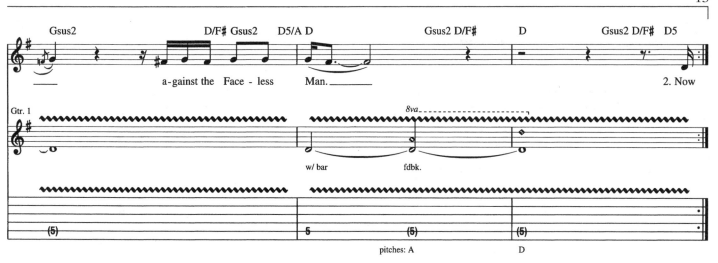

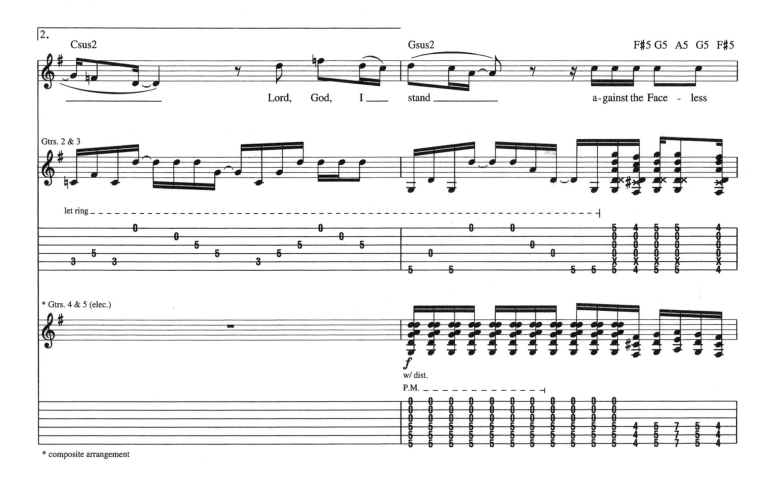

* composite arrangement

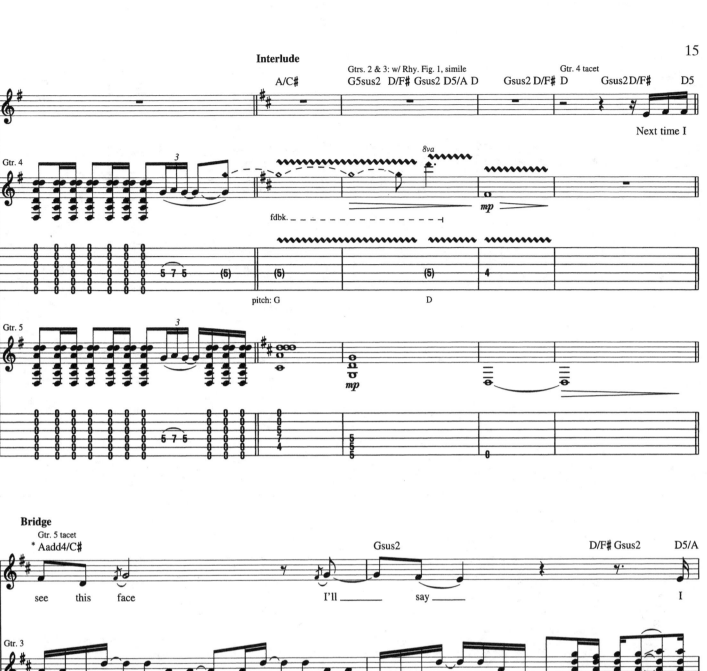

Next time I

Interlude

Bridge

Gtr. 5 tacet

* Chord symbols reflect overall tonality.

see this face I'll ___ say ___ I

choose to live for al - ways. So won't you

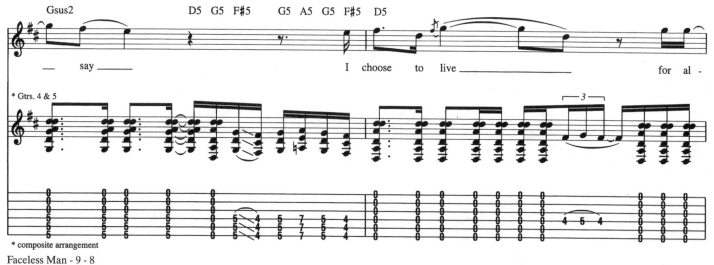

BEAUTIFUL

Words and Music by
MARK TREMONTI
and SCOTT STAPP

Drop D Tuning:
① = E ④ = D
② = B ⑤ = A
③ = G ⑥ = D

Verse
Slowly ♩ = 72

1. She wears a coat of col-or. Loved by some, feared by oth-ers. She im-mor-tal-ized in young man's eyes.
2. Lust she breeds in the eyes of broth-ers. Vi-o-lent sons make bit-ter moth-ers. Close your eyes, here's

BULLETS

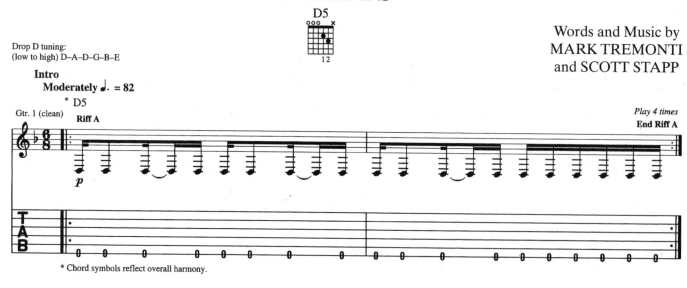

Words and Music by
MARK TREMONTI
and SCOTT STAPP

Drop D tuning:
(low to high) D–A–D–G–B–E

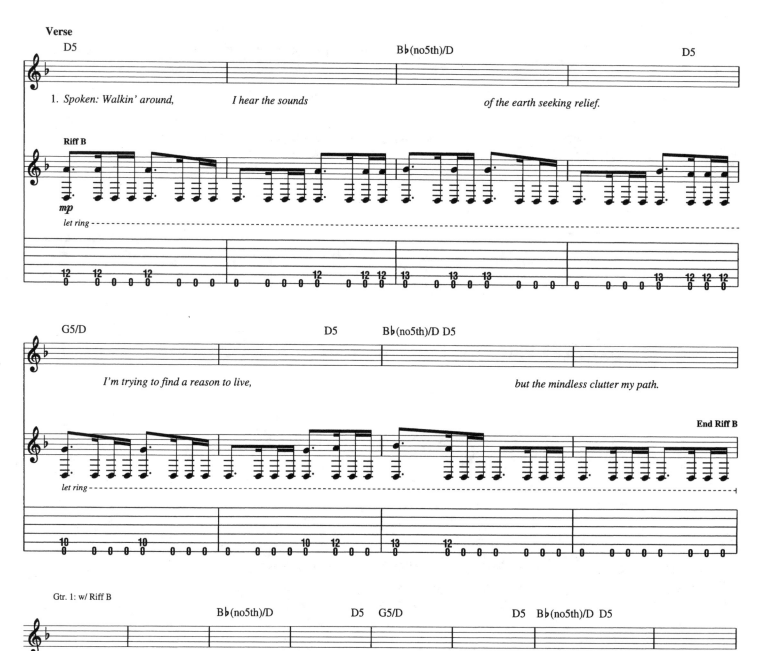

Bullets - 8 - 1

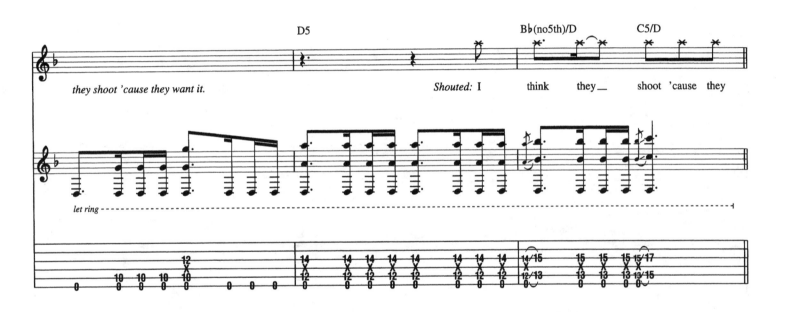

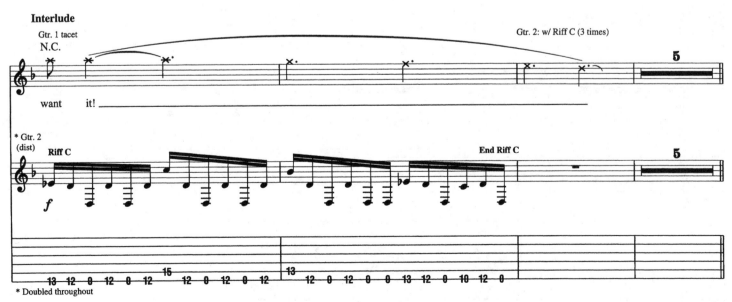

Bullets - 8 - 2

Eb5 D5 C5 D5 Eb5 D5 C5 D5 Eb5 D5 C5 D5 C5 D5
End Rhy. Fig. 2A
P.M.
End Rhy. Fig. 2
Ah.
Gtr. 1: w/ Riff A (4 times)
Gtr. 4 (dist.)
Gtr. 3 tacet
pp
w/ dist.
w/ bar
P.H.
+1/2
+1
+1 1/2
+1
-1/2
Gtrs. 2 & 3
Gtr. 2
mf
P.H.
w/ bar
-2
-1
-1
-1/2
Pitches: B G
A
B
G
G#
Bridge
Gtr. 1: w/ Riff B (2 times)
Gtr. 2 tacet
D5
Gtr. 4 tacet
Hey,
Riff E
Gtr. 3
Gtr. 2
w/ bar
P.H.
w/ bar
p
+1/2
+3/4
-1
-1/2
Pitches: A
Bb
B♮
A

all I want is what's real, some - thin' I touch and can

feel. I'll hold it close and nev - er let it go. _____ Said

End Riff E

Gtr. 3: w/ Riff E

why, _____ why do we live this life _____ with all this hate in -

D5
Gtr. 2
p

side? I'll give it a - way 'cause I don't want it no more.

Gtr. 4

w/ bar   w/ bar

-1/2

DON'T STOP DANCING

Words and Music by
MARK TREMONTI
and SCOTT STAPP

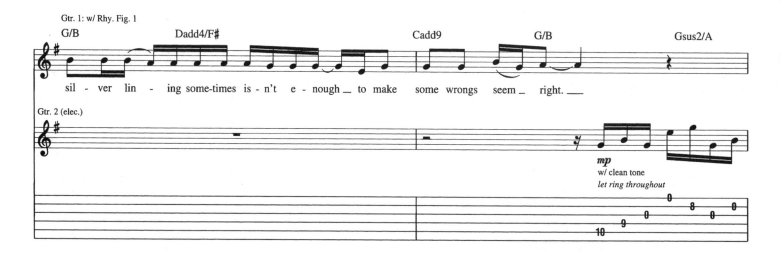

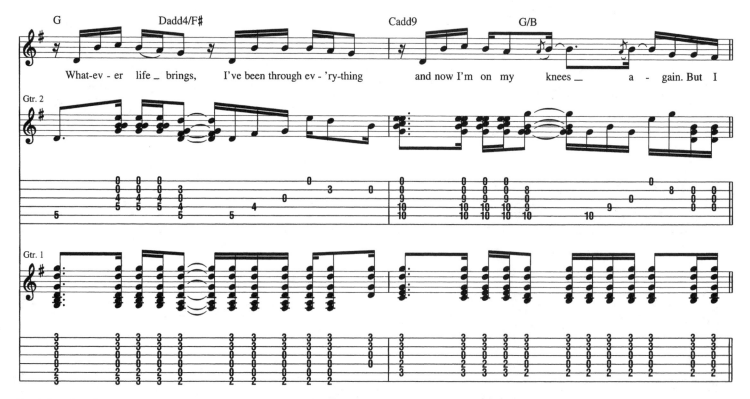

Don't Stop Dancing - 8 - 1

Pre-Chorus

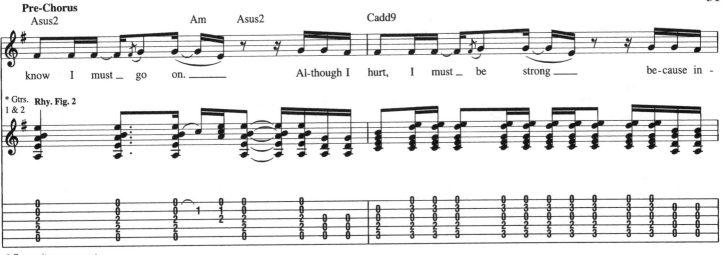

know I must __ go on. _____ Al-though I hurt, I must __ be strong _____ be-cause in -

* Composite arrangement

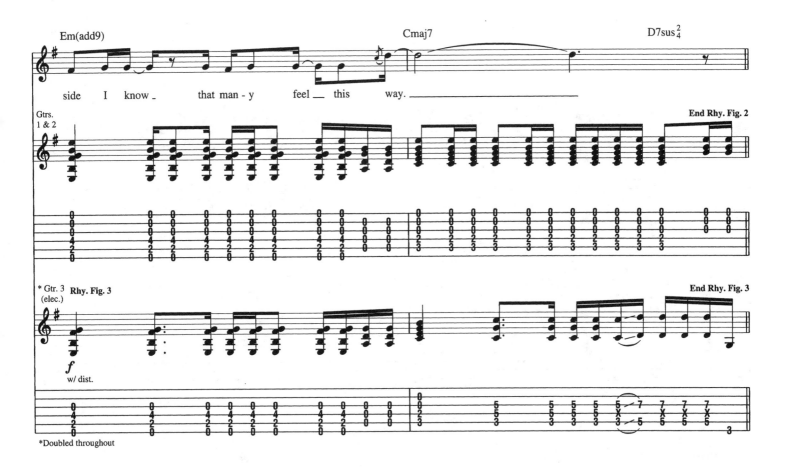

side I know __ that man - y feel __ this way. _____

*Doubled throughout

Chorus

Chil - dren, _____ don't __ stop danc - ing. _____ Be - lieve _

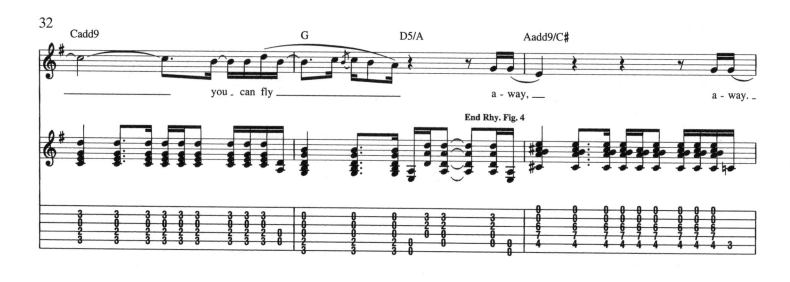

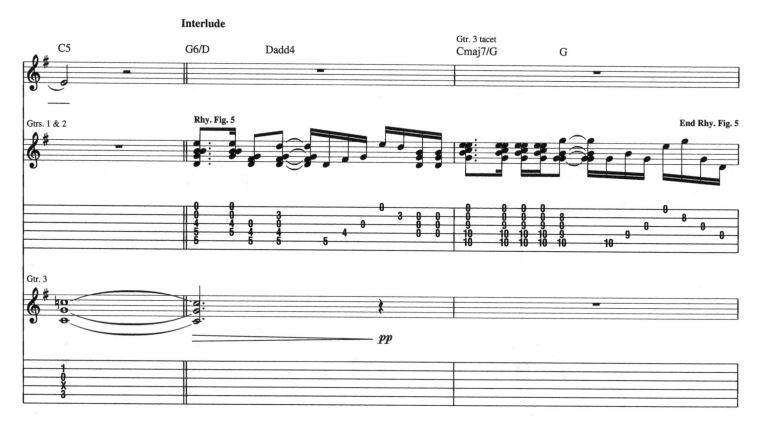

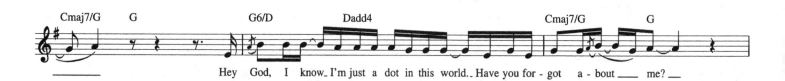

Don't Stop Dancing - 8 - 3

Pre-Chorus

know I must go on. Al-though I hurt, I must be strong because in -

side I know that man-y feel this way. **Chorus** Chil - dren, don't stop

danc - ing. Be - lieve you can fly a - way,

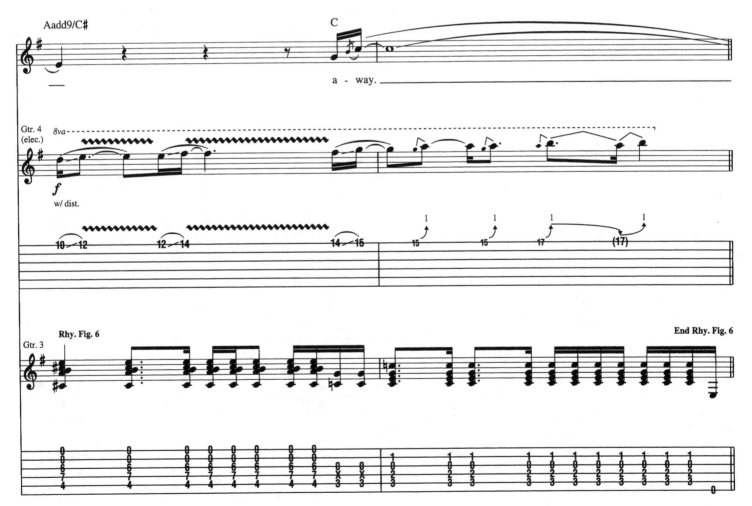

Guitar Solo

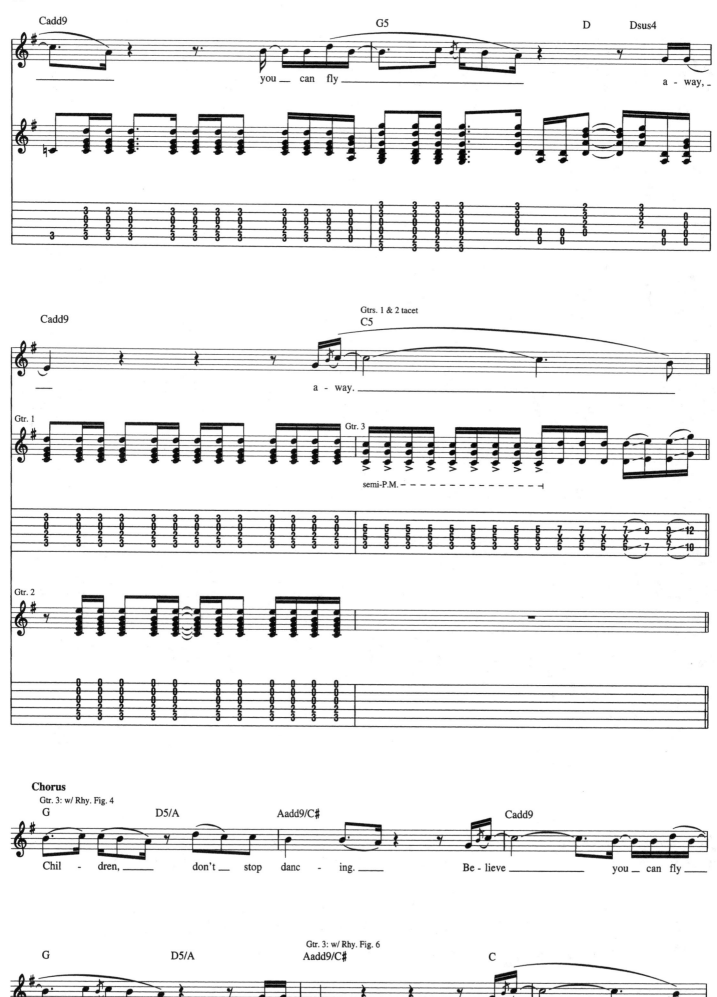

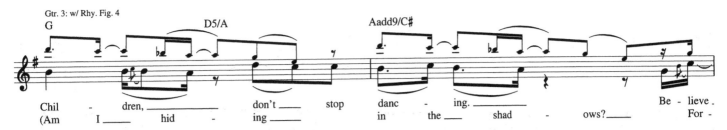

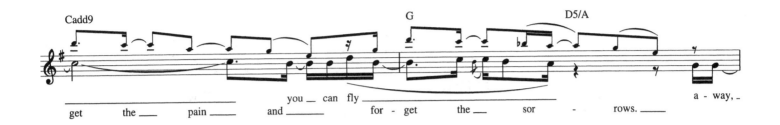

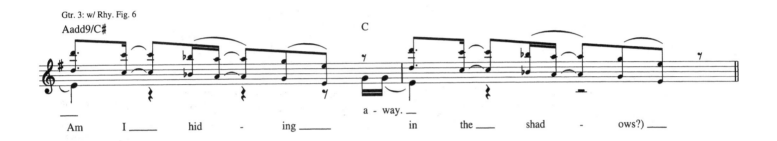

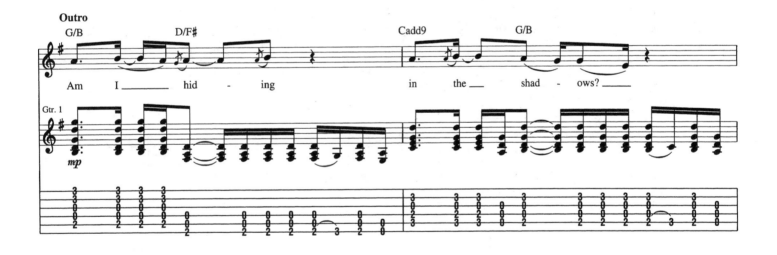

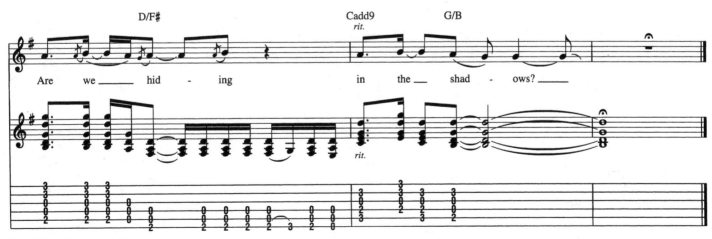

Don't Stop Dancing - 8 - 8

HIGHER

Words and Music by
MARK TREMONTI
and SCOTT STAPP

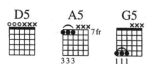

Drop D Tuning:
① = E ④ = D
② = B ⑤ = A
③ = G ⑥ = D

Intro
Slow Rock ♩ = 80

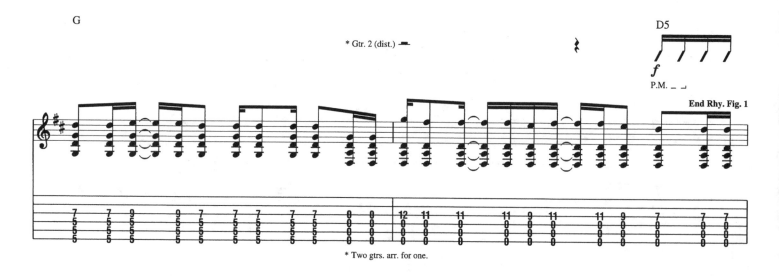

* doubled throughout ** Chord symbols reflect implied tonality.

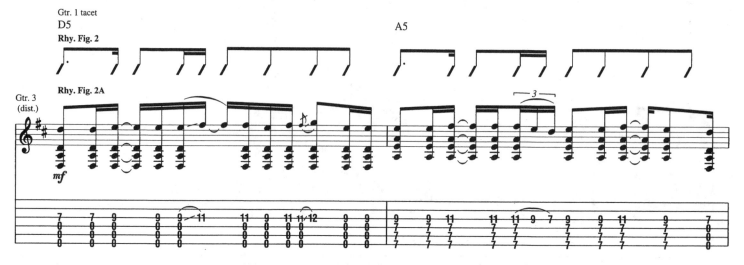

Higher - 6 - 1

IN AMERICA

Words and Music by
MARK TREMONTI
and SCOTT STAPP

In America - 6 - 1

which way _ to go. _____   I gave my last dol - lar. Can I   still come to your show? _

Gtr. 3 (elec.)

f w/ dist.

Gtr. 4 (elec.)

f w/ dist.

%§ **Chorus**

What is   right _   or wrong? _____   I don'tknow who _   to be - lieve   in.

* Gtrs.
3 & 4   **Rhy. Fig. 3**

* composite arrangement

My soul   sings a dif - 'rent song _   in A - mer - i - ca. _____

End Rhy. Fig. 3

Gtrs. 3 & 4: w/ Rhy. Fig. 3, simile

What is   right _   or wrong? _____   I don't know who _   to be - lieve   in.

To Coda ⊕

My soul   sings a dif - 'rent song _   in A - mer - i - ca, _____   in A -

In America - 6 - 6

LULLABY

Words and Music by
MARK TREMONTI and SCOTT STAPP

Gtrs. 1 & 3, Drop D tuning:
(low to high) D–A–D–G–B–E
Gtr. 2 tuning:
(low to high) E–A–D–G–B–D

Intro
Slowly ♩. = 48

*Chord symbols reflect implied harmony.

1. Hush, my love, now don't you cry. Ev - 'ry - thing will be all right. Close your eyes and drift in dream.
2. Oh, my love, in my arms tight. Ev - 'ry day you give me life. As I drift off to your world, will

Lullaby - 5 - 1

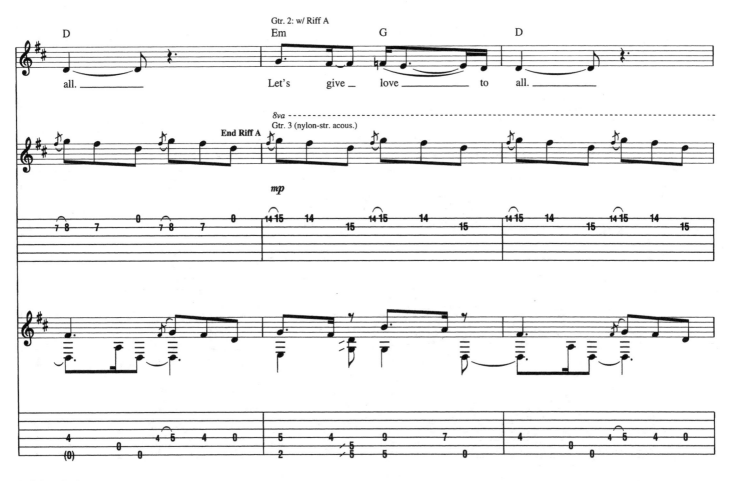

MY OWN PRISON

Words and Music by
MARK TREMONTI and SCOTT STAPP

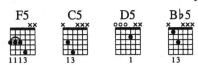

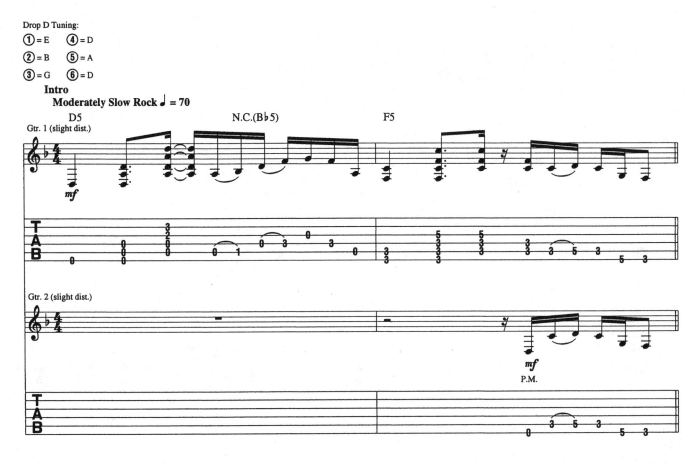

My Own Prison - 7 - 1

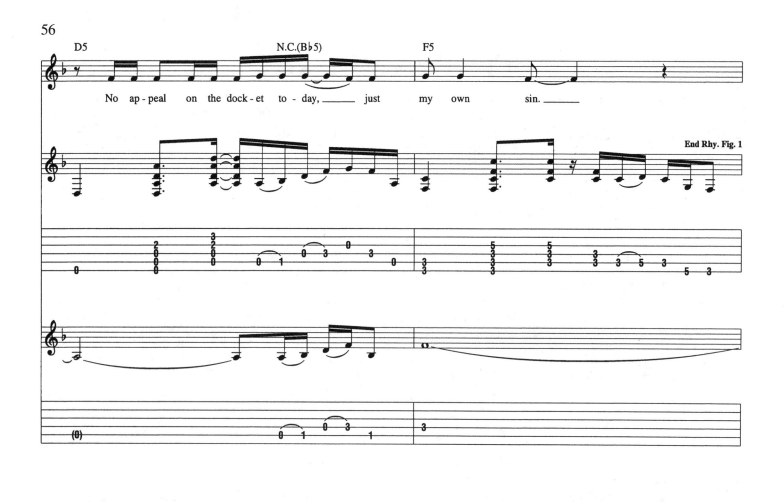

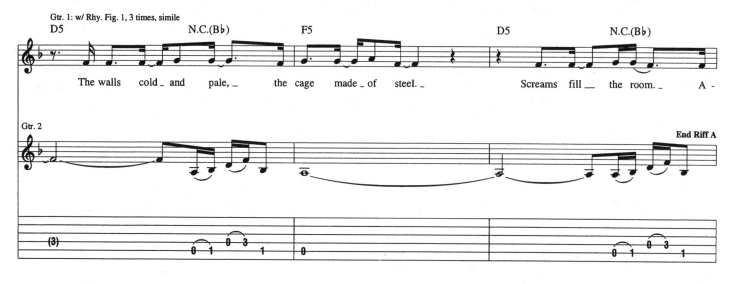

Bridge

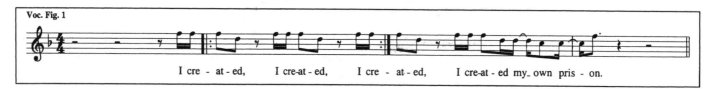

Gtr. 3: w/ Riff C, simile

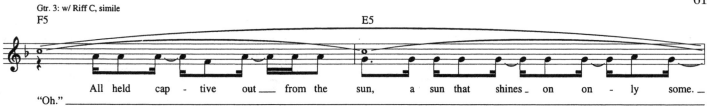

All held cap - tive out __ from the sun, a sun that shines _ on on - ly some. _

"Oh." _____

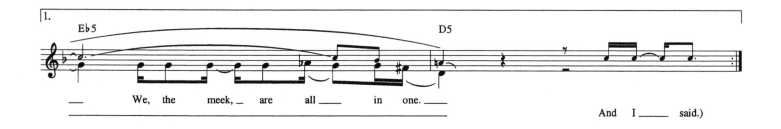

1.

__ We, the meek, _ are all __ in one. __

And I __ said.)

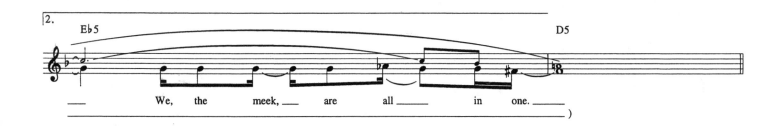

2.

__ We, the meek, __ are all ___ in one. ___)

Outro

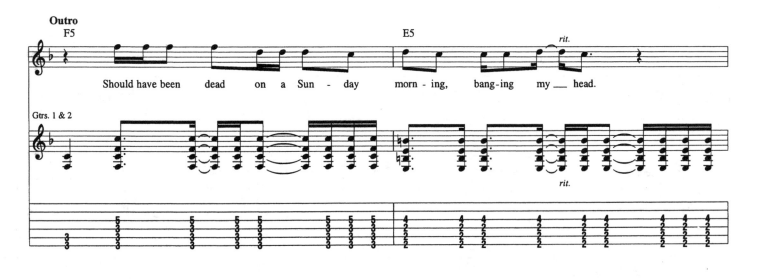

Should have been dead on a Sun - day morn - ing, bang-ing my _ head.

rit.

Gtrs. 1 & 2

rit.

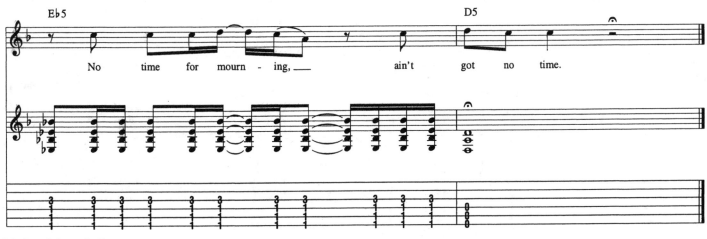

No time for mourn - ing, __ ain't got no time.

My Own Prison - 7 - 7

MY SACRIFICE

Words and Music by
MARK TREMONTI
and SCOTT STAPP

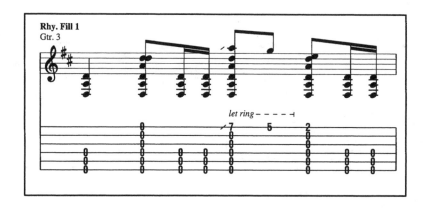

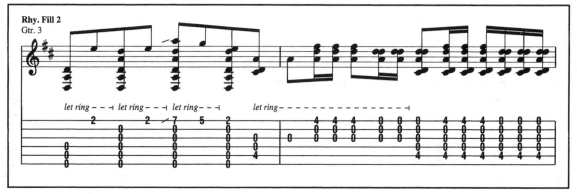

My Sacrifice - 7 - 3

Bridge

I just want to say hel - lo a - gain.

I just want to say hel - lo a - gain.

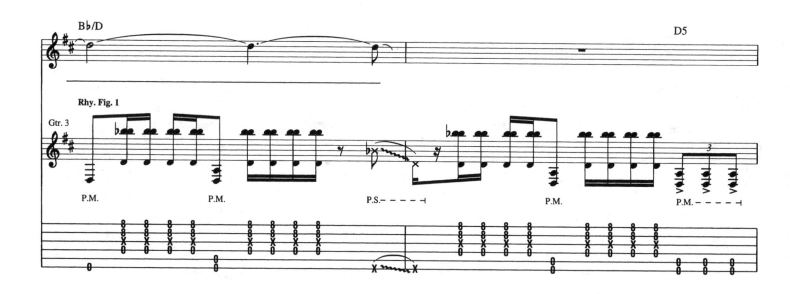

Chorus

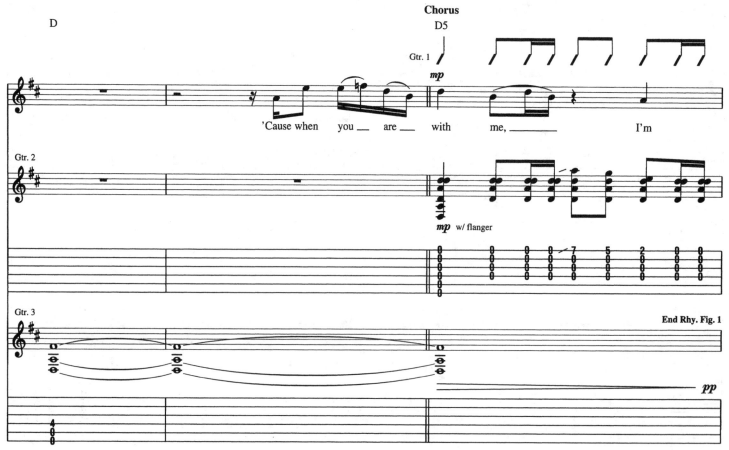

'Cause when you are with me, I'm

⊕ Coda

Bridge

Gtr. 3: w/ Riff A (3 times)

— My sac - ri - fice. ____ (I just want ___ to say ___

____ hel - lo ___ a-gain.) I ___ just want ___ to say ___ hel - lo a - gain. ___

Gtr. 3: w/ Rhy. Fig. 1

_____ My sac - ri - fice. ____

Outro

Begin fade

Gtr. 4 (elec.)

mp
w/ slight dist.
let ring throughout

Fade out

ONE

Words and Music by
MARK TREMONTI and SCOTT STAPP

* Two gtrs. arr. for one.
** Chord symbols reflect implied tonality.

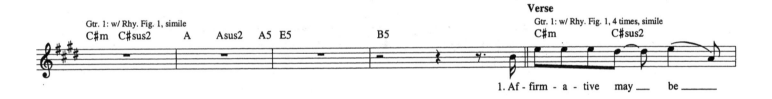

One - 5 - 1

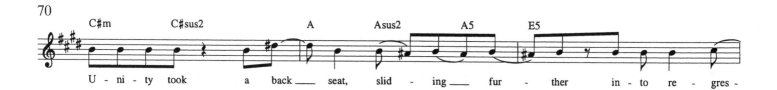

U - ni - ty took a back ___ seat, slid - ing ___ fur - ther in - to re - gres -

Pre-Chorus

Gtr. 1: w/ Rhy. Fig. 1, 2 times, simile

- sion. ___ One, ___ oh ___ one. The on - ly way ___ is one. ___

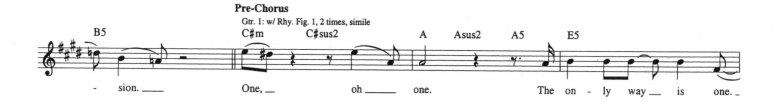

One, ___ oh ___ one. The on - ly way ___ is one. ___

%$ **Chorus**

Gtr. 3 tacet, 2nd time

I feel an - gry, ___ I feel help -

Gtr. 2 (dist.)

8va loco

Rhy. Fig. 2

Harm.*

* Position finger between 2nd & 3rd frets.

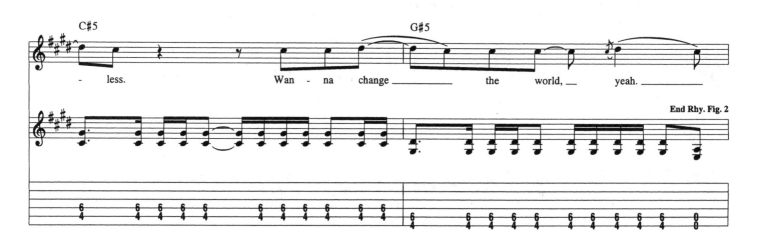

- less. Wan - na change ___ the world, ___ yeah. ___

End Rhy. Fig. 2

Gtr. 2: w/ Rhy. Fig. 2

To Coda 1 ⊕

To Coda 2 ⊕

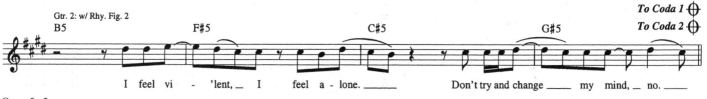

I feel vi - 'lent, ___ I feel a - lone. ___ Don't try and change ___ my mind, ___ no. ___

Interlude

Gtr. 1: w/ Rhy. Fig. 1, simile

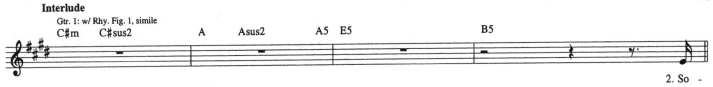

2. So -

Verse

Gtr. 1: w/ Rhy. Fig. 1, 4 times, simile

ci - e - ty blind __ by __ col - or. Why hold down one __ to raise an - oth - er? __ Dis -

crim - i - na - tion now on both __ sides, seeds __ of __ hate __ blos-som fur - ther. __ The

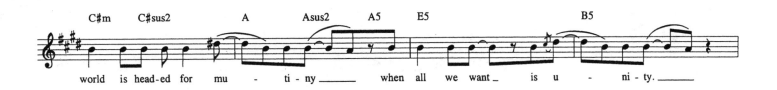

world is head-ed for mu - ti - ny _____ when all we want __ is u - ni - ty. _____

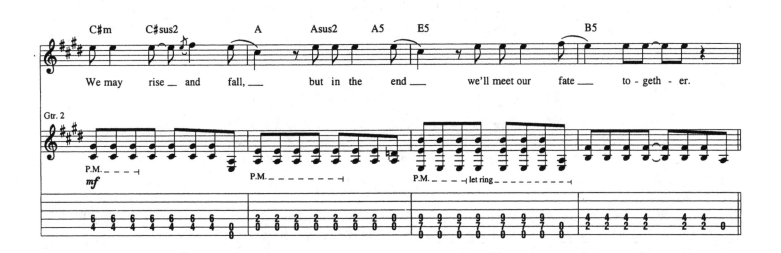

We may rise __ and fall, __ but in the end __ we'll meet our fate __ to-geth - er.

Pre-Chorus

Gtr. 1: w/ Rhy. Fig. 1, 2 times, simile

One, _ oh ___ one. The on - ly way __ is one. __

One - 5 - 3

One, ___ oh ___ one. The on - ly way ___ is one. ___

⊕ Coda 1

Chorus

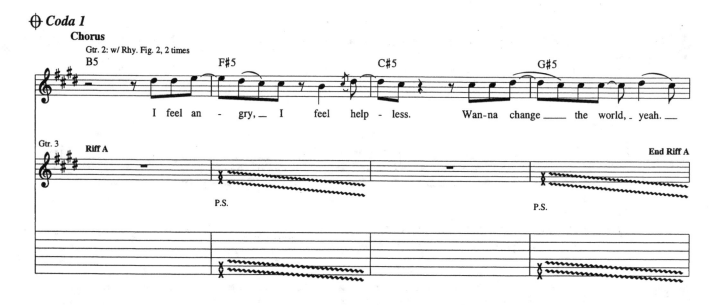

I feel an - gry, ___ I feel help - less. Wan-na change ___ the world, ___ yeah.

I feel vi - 'lent, I feel a - lone. _____ Don't try and change ___ my mind, _ no. _____

Bridge

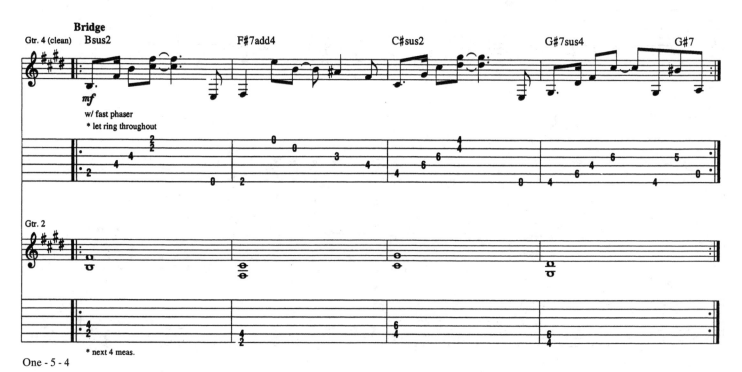

One - 5 - 5

ONE LAST BREATH

Words and Music by
MARK TREMONTI
and SCOTT STAPP

Intro
Slowly ♩ = 63

*Chord symbols reflect implied harmony.

Verse
Gtr. 1: w/ Riff A (2 times)

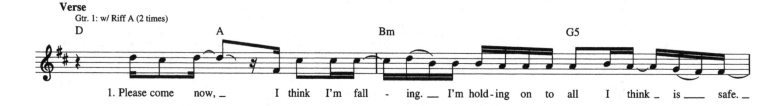

1. Please come now, __ I think I'm fall - ing. __ I'm hold-ing on to all I think __ is __ safe. __

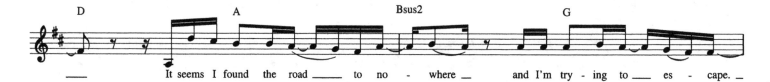

__ It seems I found the road __ to no - where __ and I'm try - ing to __ es - cape. __

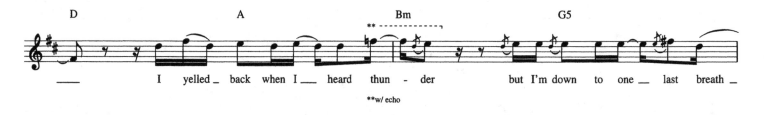

__ I yelled __ back when I __ heard thun - der __ but I'm down to one __ last breath __

**w/ echo

__ and with it, let __ me say, __ let me say...

One Last Breath - 6 - 1

Chorus

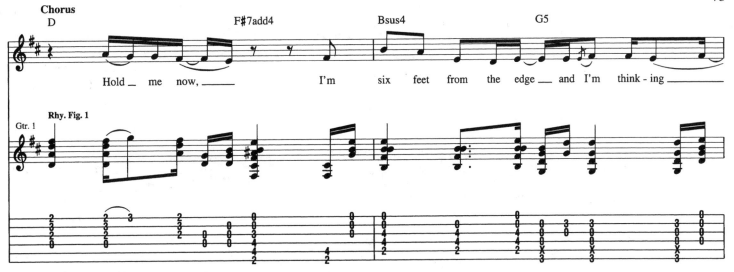

Hold __ me now, _____ I'm six feet from the edge __ and I'm think-ing ____

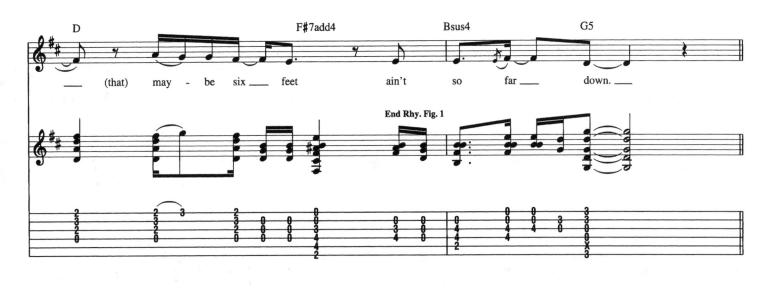

__ (that) may - be six __ feet ain't so far __ down. __

Interlude

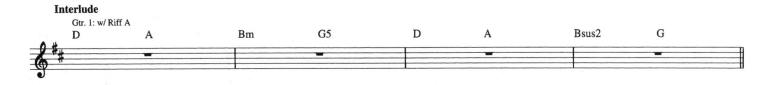

Verse

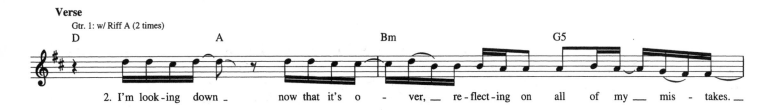

2. I'm look-ing down __ now that it's o - ver, __ re - flect-ing on all of my __ mis - takes. __

__ I thought I found __ the road __ to some - where, __ some - where __ in __ His __ grace. __

One Last Breath - 6 - 2

One Last Breath - 6 - 4

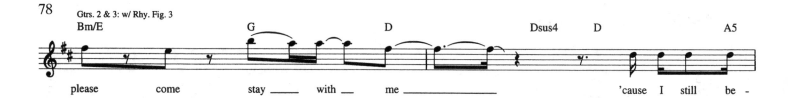

please come stay ___ with ___ me _____ 'cause I still be -

lieve ___ there's some - thing left ___ for you and me, for you and me, for you and me. ___

Interlude

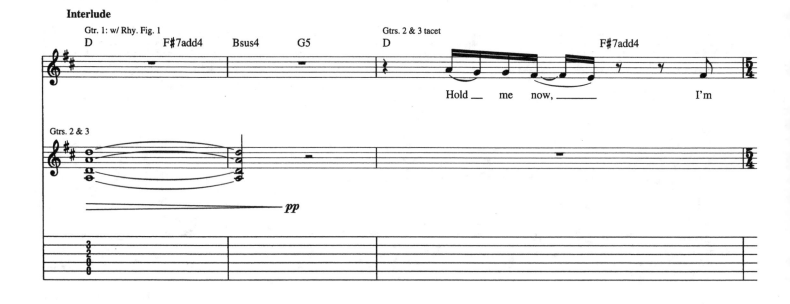

Hold ___ me now, _____ I'm

D.S. al Coda

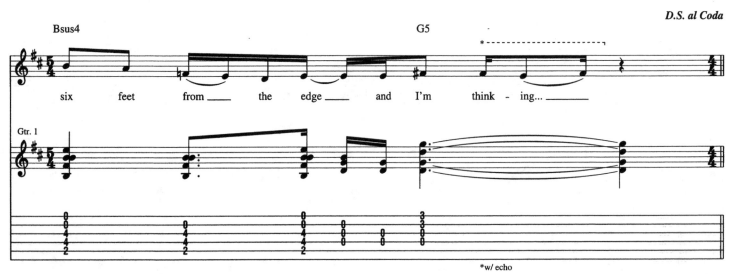

six feet from ___ the edge ___ and I'm think - ing... _____

*w/ echo

⊕ Coda

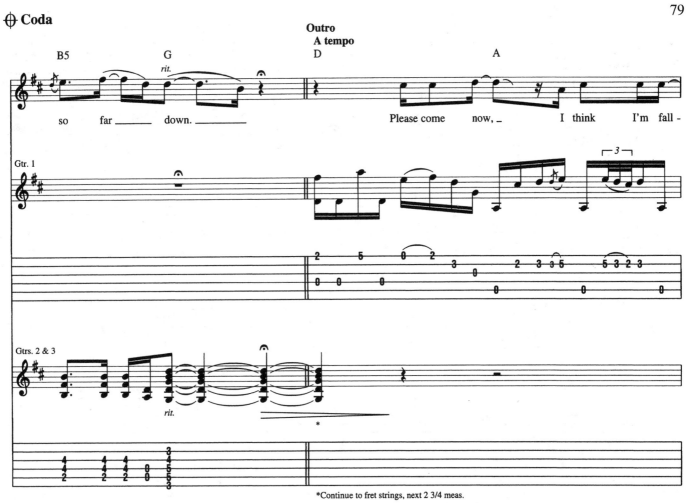

*Continue to fret strings, next 2 3/4 meas.

so far _____ down. _____ Please come now, ___ I think I'm fall-

-ing. ___ I'm hold-ing on to all I think ___ is safe. _____

PITY FOR A DIME

Words and Music by
MARK TREMONTI
and SCOTT STAPP

Pity for a Dime - 6 - 1

Sell my pi - ty for __ a dime, __ yeah, __ just one __ dime. __

Interlude

Gtrs. 1 & 2 Rhy. Fig. 3

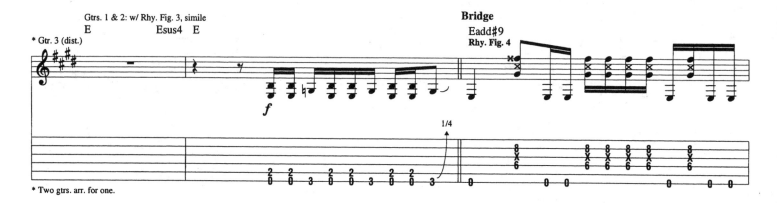

Gtrs. 1 & 2: w/ Rhy. Fig. 3, simile

* Gtr. 3 (dist.)

Bridge

* Two gtrs. arr. for one.

Plain __

talk __ can be __ the eas - y way. __

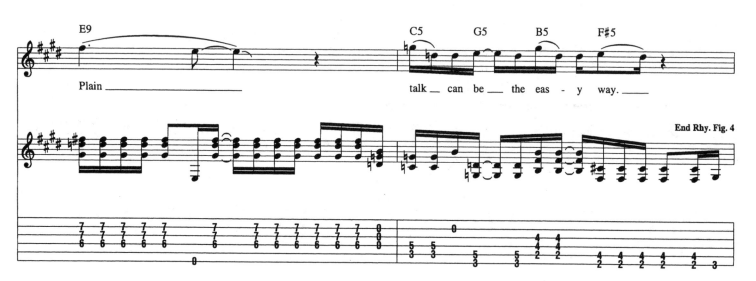

Gtr. 3: w/ Rhy. Fig. 4, 2 times, simile

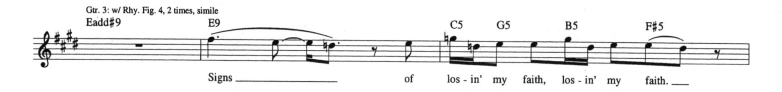

Signs __ of los - in' my faith, los - in' my faith. __

Plain __ talk __ can be __ the eas - y way. __

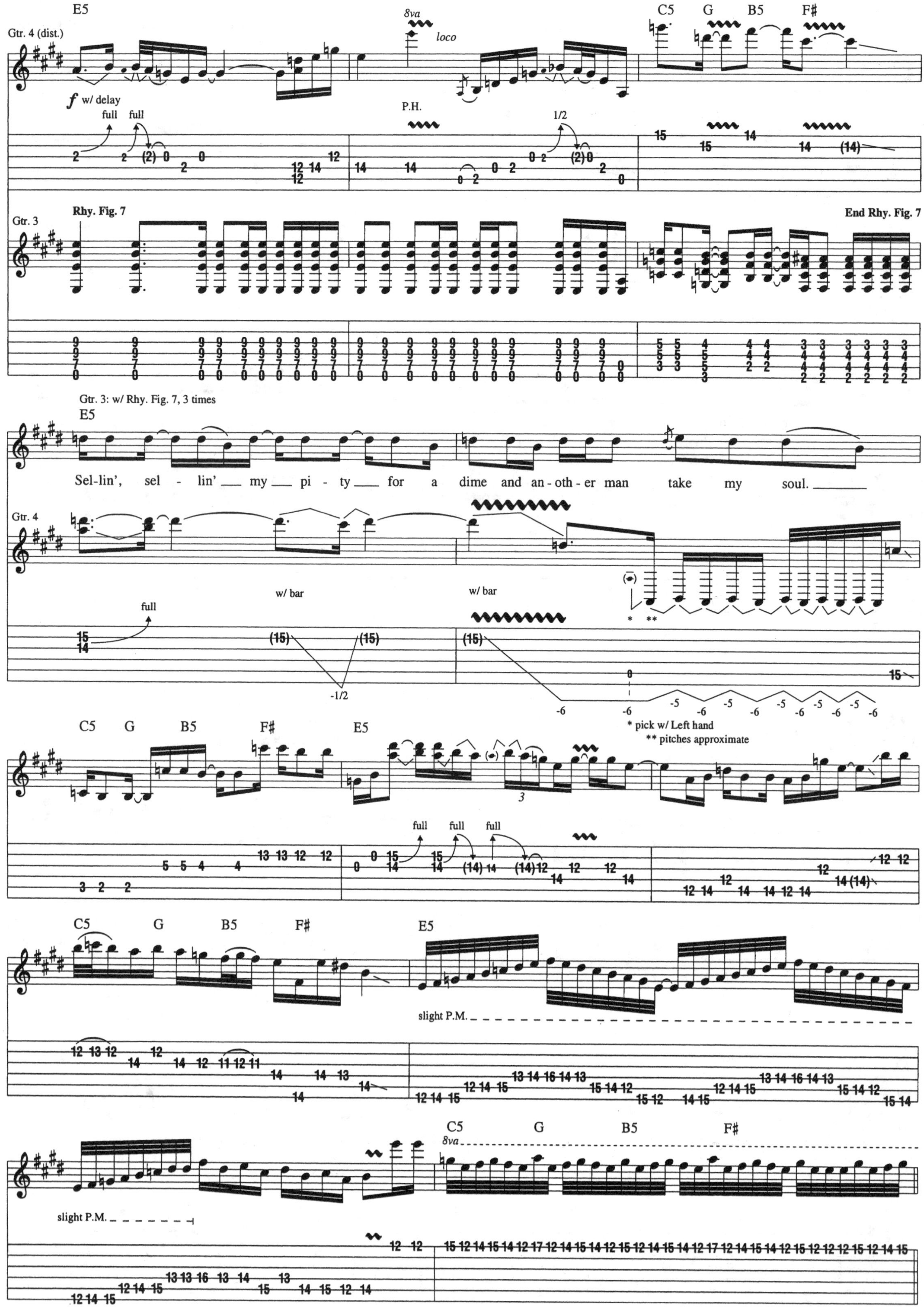
E5
Gtr. 4 (dist.)
8va
loco
C5 G B5 F♯
f w/ delay
full full
P.H.
1/2
Gtr. 3
Rhy. Fig. 7
End Rhy. Fig. 7
Gtr. 3: w/ Rhy. Fig. 7, 3 times
Sel-lin', sel - lin' my pi - ty for a dime and an-oth-er man take my soul.
Gtr. 4
w/ bar
full
-1/2
* pick w/ Left hand
** pitches approximate
slight P.M.

Chorus

So I sat down for a while, _____ yeah, _____ forc - in' a smile. _____

Coda

Outro

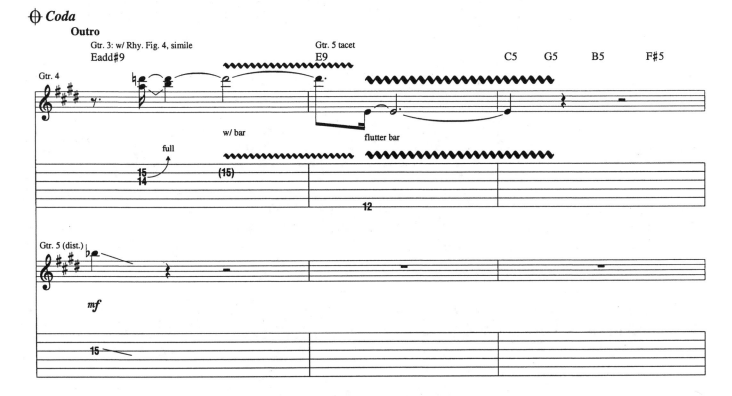

Sell - in', sell - in' ___ my ___ pit - y ___ for a dime and an - oth - er man take my soul. ___

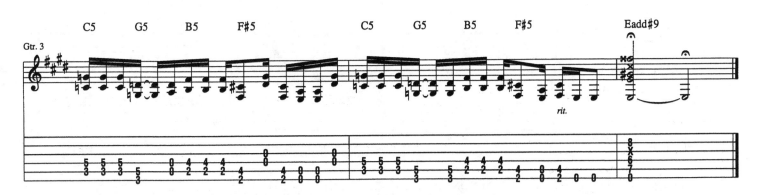

Pity for a Dime - 6 - 6

TORN

Words and Music by
MARK TREMONTI
and SCOTT STAPP

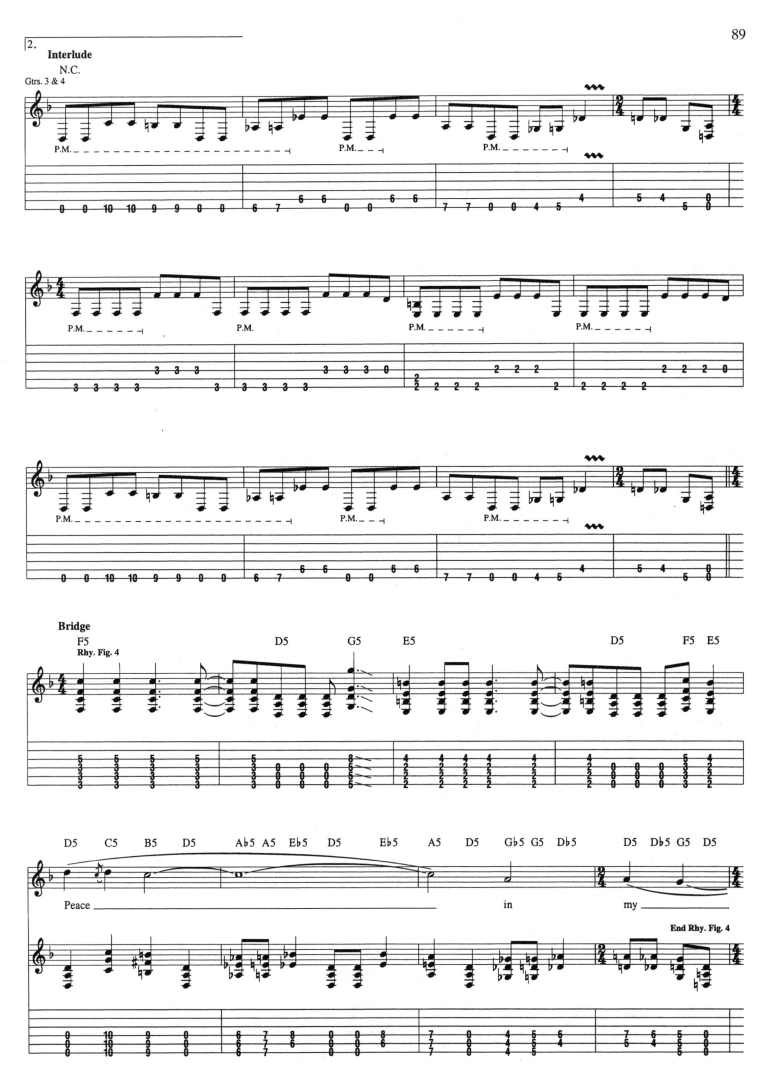

Outro

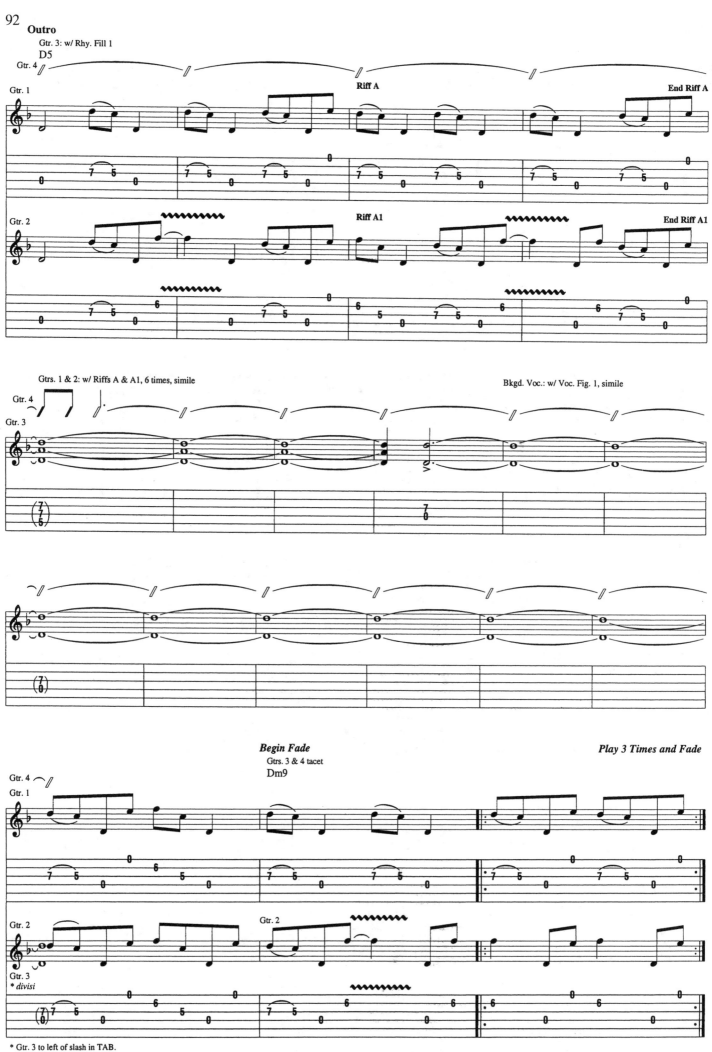

WEATHERED

Words and Music by
MARK TREMONTI and SCOTT STAPP

Weathered - 11 - 1

95

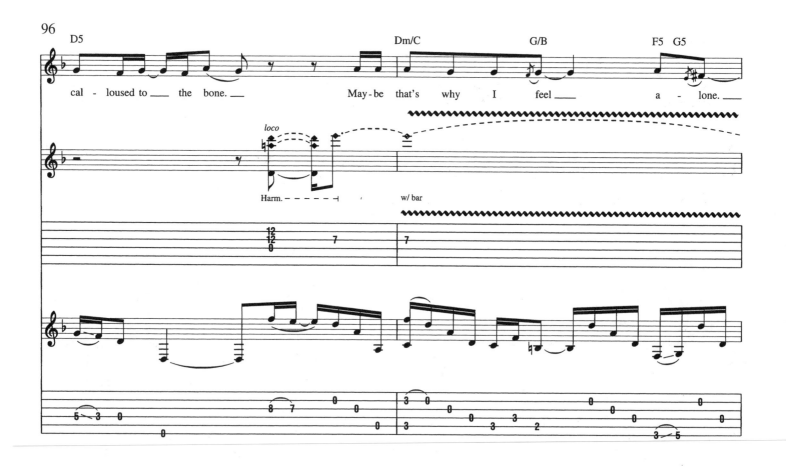

Some-times I feel __ like __ giv-ing up. _____ Yeah I said __

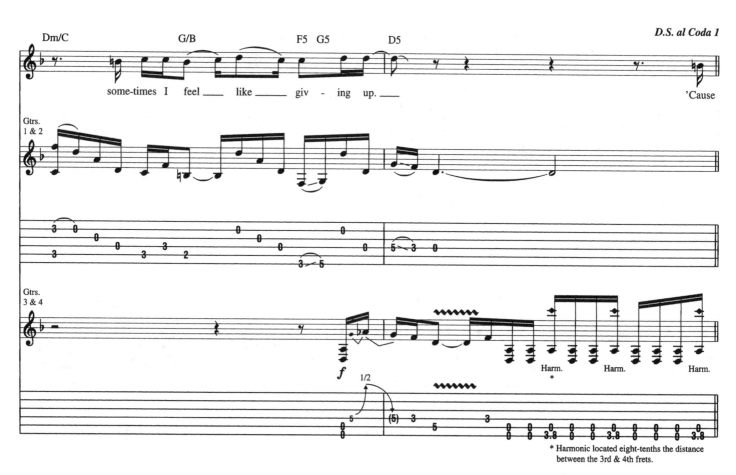

D.S. al Coda 1

some-times I feel ____ like _____ giv - ing up. ____ 'Cause

Gtrs.
1 & 2

Gtrs.
3 & 4

Harm.
*

Harm.

Harm.

* Harmonic located eight-tenths the distance
between the 3rd & 4th frets.

Coda 1

Interlude

heal. _____ It just won't

WHAT'S THIS LIFE FOR

Words and Music by
MARK TREMONTI
and SCOTT STAPP

Intro
Moderately Slow ♩ = 70

* Chord symbols reflect implied tonality.

Rhy. Fig. 1

End Rhy. Fig. 1

Verse
Gtr. 1: w/ Rhy. Fig. 1, 3 1/2 times

1. Hur-ray ___ for _____ a child _ that makes _ it through. ___ If there's an-y way, _ be-cause

the an - swer lies ___ in you. ___ They're laid to rest ___ be-fore

they've known _ just what _ to do. ___ Their souls are lost ___ be - cause

Chorus

they could nev - er find. ___
you could nev - er find. ___

What's this life _____ for? _____

* Gtr. 2 (elec.)

* Two gtrs. arr. for one.

What's This Life For - 6 - 1

What's this life ___ for? ___

What's this life ___ for? ___

To Coda ⊕

What's this life ___ for? ___

Interlude
Gtr. 2 tacet

* Gtr. 1

* doubled

106

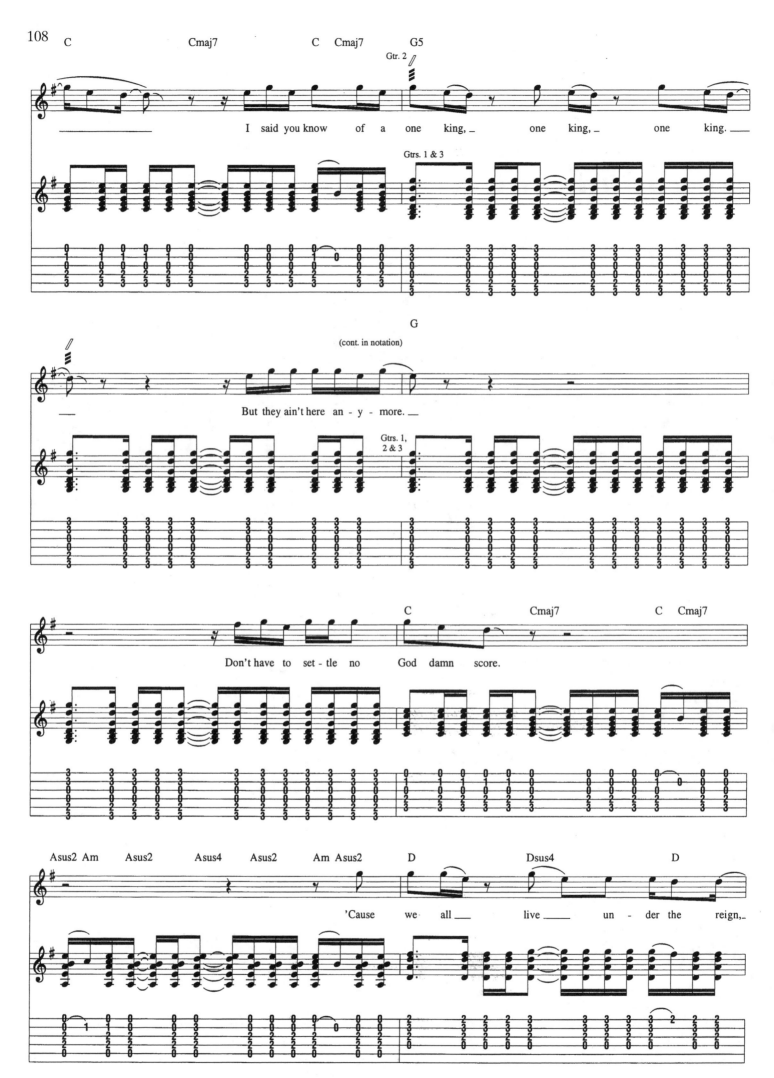

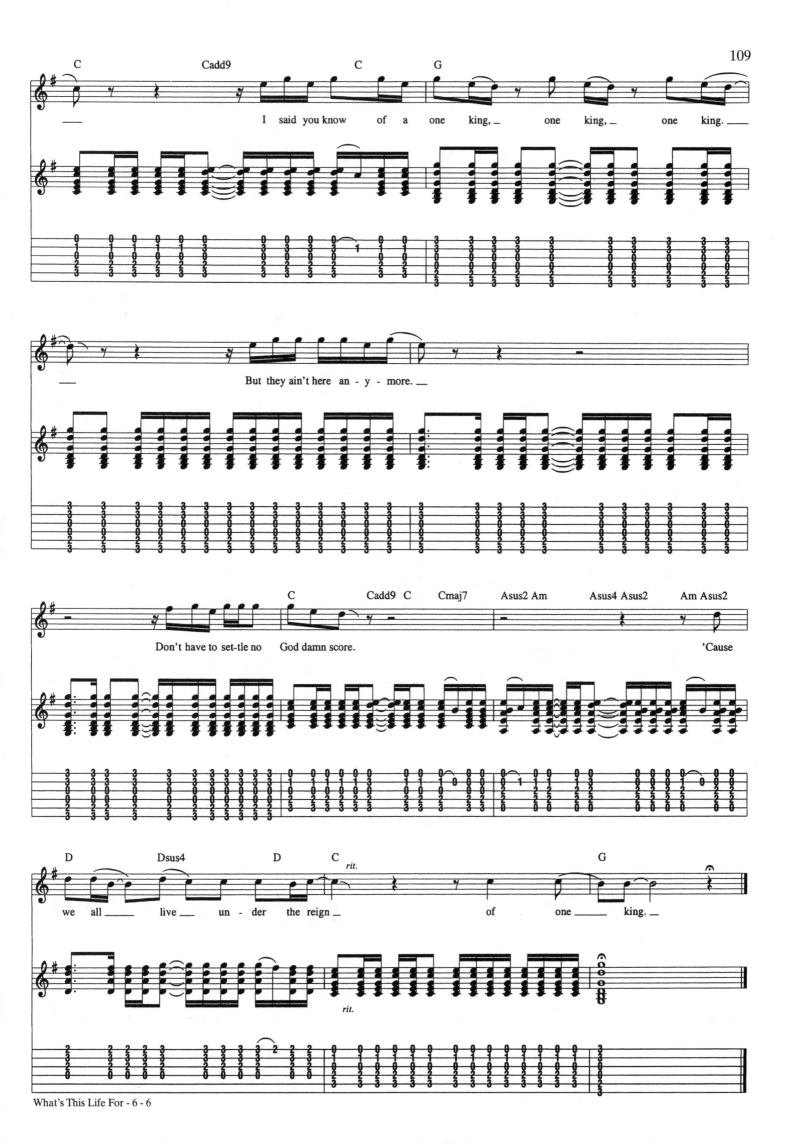

WITH ARMS WIDE OPEN

Words and Music by
MARK TREMONTI
and **SCOTT STAPP**

© 1999 TREMONTI/STAPP MUSIC (BMI) and FSMGI (IMRO)
All Rights Administered by STATE ONE MUSIC AMERICA (BMI)
All Rights Reserved

With Arms Wide Open - 8 - 1

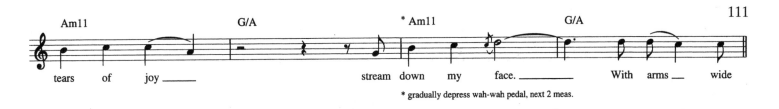

tears of joy _____ stream down my face. _____ With arms _____ wide

gradually depress wah-wah pedal, next 2 meas.

Chorus

o - pen, _____ un - der _____ the sun - light. _____ Wel - come

* Gtrs. 2 & 3 (clean)

mf

* composite arrangement

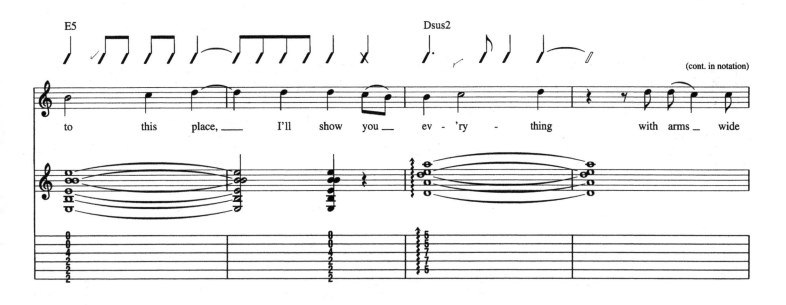

(cont. in notation)

to this place, _____ I'll show you _____ ev - 'ry - thing with arms _ wide

Gtr. 3 tacet

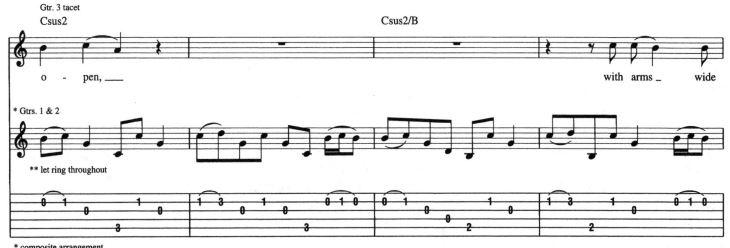

o - pen, _____ with arms _ wide

* Gtrs. 1 & 2

** let ring throughout

* composite arrangement
** next 8 meas.

With Arms Wide Open - 8 - 2

WHAT IF

Words and Music by
MARK TREMONTI and SCOTT STAPP

What If - 5 - 1

Verse

Gtr. 1 tacet

N.C.(D5)   (B♭5)   (E5)   D5   N.C.(B♭5)   (E5)

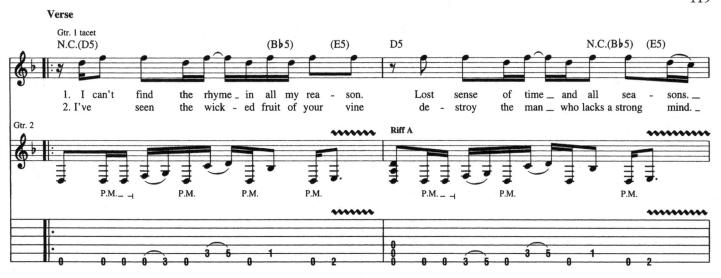

1. I can't find the rhyme in all my rea - son.   Lost sense of time and all sea - sons.
2. I've seen the wick - ed fruit of your vine   de - stroy the man who lacks a strong mind.

Gtr. 2

Riff A

P.M.   P.M.   P.M.   P.M.   P.M.   P.M.   P.M.

D5   N.C.(B♭5)   (E5)   D5   N.C.(B♭5)   N.C.

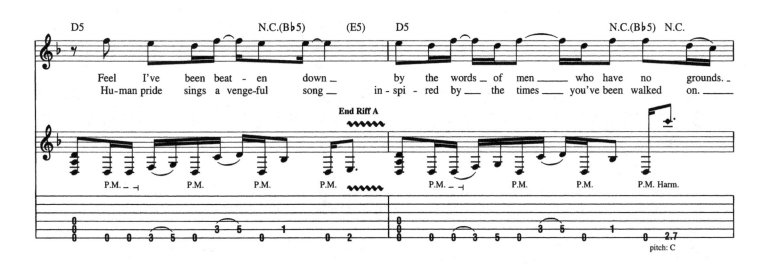

Feel I've been beat - en down by the words of men who have no grounds.
Hu - man pride sings a venge - ful song in - spi - red by the times you've been walked on.

End Riff A

P.M.   P.M.   P.M.   P.M.   P.M.   P.M.   P.M.   P.M. Harm.

pitch: C

Gtr. 2: w/ Riff A, 2 times, 1st time; 1 1/2 times, 2nd time

D5   N.C.(B♭5)   (E5)   D5   N.C.(B♭5)   (E5)

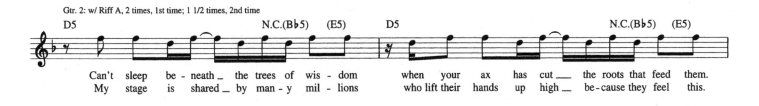

Can't sleep be - neath the trees of wis - dom when your ax has cut the roots that feed them.
My stage is shared by man - y mil - lions who lift their hands up high be - cause they feel this.

Gtr. 2: w/ Fill 1, 2nd time

D5   N.C.(B♭5)   E5   D5   N.C.(B♭5)   E5

Forked tongues in bit - ter mouths can drive a man to bleed from in - side out.
We are one, we are strong. The more you hold us down the more we press on.

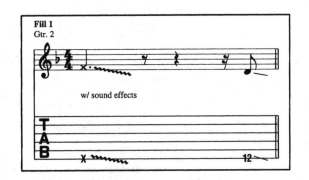

Fill 1
Gtr. 2

w/ sound effects

What If - 5 - 3

TABLATURE EXPLANATION

TAB illustrates the six strings of the guitar.
Notes and chords are indicated by the placement of fret numbers on each string.

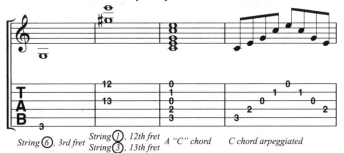

String ⑥, 3rd fret   *String ①, 12th fret*   *A "C" chord*   *C chord arpeggiated*
                      String ③, 13th fret

BENDING NOTES

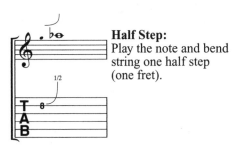

Half Step:
Play the note and bend string one half step (one fret).

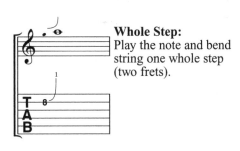

Whole Step:
Play the note and bend string one whole step (two frets).

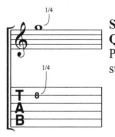

**Slight Bend/
Quarter-Tone Bend:**
Play the note and bend string sharp.

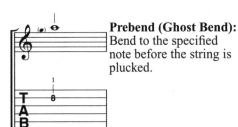

Prebend (Ghost Bend):
Bend to the specified note before the string is plucked.

Prebend and Release:
Play the already-bent string, then immediately drop it down to the fretted note.

Unison Bends:
Play both notes and immediately bend the lower note to the same pitch as the higher note.

Bend and Release:
Play the note and bend to the next pitch, then release to the original note. Only the first note is attacked.

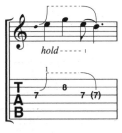

Bends Involving More Than One String:
Play the note and bend the string while playing an additional note on another string. Upon release, relieve the pressure from the additional note allowing the original note to sound alone.

Bends Involving Stationary Notes:
Play both notes and immediately bend the lower note up to pitch. Return as indicated.

ARTICULATIONS

Hammer On:
Play the lower note, then "hammer" your finger to the higher note. Only the first note is plucked.

Pull Off:
Play the higher note with your first finger already in position on the lower note. Pull your finger off the first note with a strong downward motion that plucks the string—sounding the lower note.

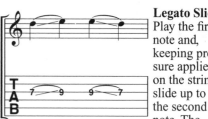

Legato Slide:
Play the first note and, keeping pressure applied on the string, slide up to the second note. The diagonal line shows that it is a slide and not a hammer-on or a pull-off.

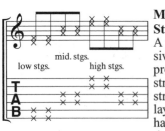

Muted Strings:
A percussive sound is produced by striking the strings while laying the fret hand across them.

Palm Mute:
The notes are muted (muffled) by placing the palm of the pick hand lightly on the strings, just in front of the bridge.

HARMONICS

Natural Harmonic:
A finger of the fret hand lightly touches the string at the note indicated in the TAB and is plucked by the pick producing a bell-like sound called a harmonic.

RHYTHM SLASHES

Strum Marks/ Rhythm Slashes:
Strum with the indicated rhythm pattern. Strum marks can be located above the staff or within the staff.

Single Notes with Rhythm Slashes:
Sometimes single notes are incorporated into a strum pattern. The circled number below is the string and the fret number is above.

Artificial Harmonic:
Fret the note at the first TAB number, lightly touch the string at the fret indicated in parens (usually 12 frets higher than the fretted note), then pluck the string with an available finger or your pick.

TREMOLO BAR

Specified Interval:
The pitch of a note or chord is lowered to the specified interval and then return as indicated. The action of the tremolo bar is graphically represented by the peaks and valleys of the diagram.

Unspecified Interval:
The pitch of a note or chord is lowered, usually very dramatically, until the pitch of the string becomes indeterminate.

PICK DIRECTION

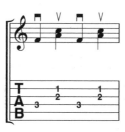

Downstrokes and Upstrokes:
The downstroke is indicated with this symbol (⊓) and the upstroke is indicated with this (∨).